HOW TO PAINT
A VERMEER

GEORGE DEEM

Introduction by Robert Rosenblum

HOW TO PAINT A VERMEER

A Painter's History of Art

with 94 illustrations, 91 in color

 Thames & Hudson

page 2: *Sebastian in the Kitchen*
(detail), 1977 (see pp. 50–51)
This page: *Everybody's Schoolroom*
(detail), 1994 (see pp. 108–9)

© 2004 George Deem
Introductory text © 2004 Robert Rosenblum

First published in 2004 in paperback in the
United States of America by Thames & Hudson Inc.,
500 Fifth Avenue, New York, New York 10110

thamesandhudsonusa.com

Library of Congress Catalog Card Number
2004100753

ISBN 0-500-28509-8

Printed and bound in China by C & C Offset

CONTENTS

GEORGE DEEM: THE ART OF ART HISTORY
by Robert Rosenblum

From the 1960s on, the three tenses of modern art – past, present, future – began to be shuffled in unexpected ways. For the heroic early decades of the last century, to be a modern artist generally meant keeping one's eyes straight ahead, as if predicting the next stage in a Darwinian evolution. The abiding imperative was to shed the past, because the present had become so excitingly unfamiliar, and the future would be even more so. Sometimes this historical house-cleaning was done in a spirit of violent revolt, as in the case of the mechanical uproars of Italian Futurism or of the clean abstract slates proposed by Russian artists fired by the events of 1917. Sometimes it was done more peacefully, inside the artists' ivory towers, as in the case of the emergence of Cubism or of an art, like Kandinsky's and Mondrian's, that finally dissolved the visible world. But whatever its variations, the over-riding impulse was to confront an ever newer art that, either respectfully or angrily, would bury earlier centuries. It was a religion of perpetual change, of youthful hopes for a different and better world.

In the last third of the century, these directions changed drastically, as if the muse of progress had been replaced by a rear-view mirror. Already in the 1960s, artists like Lichtenstein had begun to make visual jokes on the sacrosanct history of modern art's pioneering adventures, and with smiles on their faces, turned the pieties of modernism, encapsulated in New York's Museum of Modern Art, into a quaint old period style that seemed as remote from the present as Neoclassicism. More and more, in fact, artists began to look backwards rather than forwards. The burdens of art history, presumably irrelevant to the future on the horizon, became inspirations once again; and in architecture as well as in painting, the huge voids left by modernism's censorship of the past were rapidly filled with a new delight in looking at the art of earlier centuries. Whether a world of classical architectural orders or of realist painting in museums, art history began to live in the present tense. By 1978, in fact, these enjoyable retrospections had become so much a part of younger artists' repertories that the Whitney Museum of American Art could organize an exhibition titled "Art about Art," where artists of many different stripes – Andy Warhol, George Segal, Robert Colescott, Larry Rivers, Peter Saul, among others – were shown together, united by their common fascination with the art-historical past and their efforts to resurrect it in a variety of unexpected ways. The elemental, history-defying purities of the ancestral figures of modern art made an about-face, and the suppressed memories of the bastions of tradition – museums, survey courses, textbooks – suddenly flooded the new and now very impure spaces of contemporary art.

George Deem, who had been working in this vein
since the 1960s, was very much part of the show,
represented by two variations on paintings by the artist
who, over the decades, has never stopped obsessing him,
Jan Vermeer. Although the two canvases were included
in a group of other artists' variations on Vermeer, they
immediately proclaimed a different vision. Malcolm
Morley, for one, was represented by his replication of a
Vermeer classic, the *Artist in His Studio* (Vienna), but
he reproduced it with a white margin, postcard-style,
in order to emphasize the fact that his handmade work
was a reproduction of a reproduction, a feat he had
also performed with Raphael's *School of Athens*, another
painting in Deem's repertory. As for Joseph Cornell,
his homage to Vermeer, one of many from the 1950s,
took the form of a pale, scrapbook-like cut-out of the
figure in *The Woman with the Pearl Earring*. In Cornell's
hands, this diminutive, withered souvenir becomes a
Proustian madeleine.

Deem, of course, was also infatuated with Vermeer,
but in this company, his singularity became, if anything,
even more pronounced. In the two works exhibited,
George Washington Vermeer (1974) and *Vermeer Interior*
(1976), Deem displayed another kind of relationship to
the great painter, one which echoes the legend of the
sculptor Pygmalion who became enamoured of the ivory
sculpture he had carved of a woman. The statue was
then magically brought to life by Venus and, now
recreated in living and breathing flesh, got to be
named Galatea.

This, in a way, is what Deem does not only to
Vermeer, but to the entire museum repertory, from the
Quattrocento right up to Hans Hofmann and Ed Ruscha.
But the Dutch master is the painter's special Galatea,
whose muse has presided over Deem's work for four
decades, right into the twenty-first century with two
exhibitions that continued to worship at this shrine:
in 2002, "Vermeer Extended" (New York, Pavel Zoubok
Gallery); and in 2003, "Paintings of Vermeer Interiors"
(Yale University, Jonathan Edwards College Master's
House). For Deem, Vermeer's domestic spaces can be
magically transformed into an imagined reality, the
equivalent of a stage set in which furniture can be moved
about and a changing cast of characters can enact their
quiet dramas or even disappear entirely, leaving behind
only a virginal, a chair, or a table. And if they are fluid in
their interior spaces, furnishings, and occupants, they are
also fluid in time and geography. For example, in *George
Washington Vermeer* (see p. 87), one of the two paintings
at the 1978 Whitney exhibition, Vermeer's lady at the
virginal and her gentleman companion have, like actors,
made an exit, leaving the room almost, but not quite,
intact. In place of the framed mirror over the virginal,
there now hangs one of Gilbert Stuart's famous portraits
of George Washington, a quietly Magritte-like intrusion
that nevertheless makes some historical sense, wedding
as it does the seventeenth-century Dutch Republic to its
early history in the American Colonies. And an even
more extreme example of time-travel is found in the 1979
diptych, *New York Artist in His Studio/Vermeer's "Artist in*

His Studio" (see pp. 64–65). Here, Deem offers another transatlantic voyage of the imagination. One of the pair is a life-size replica of Vermeer's renowned view of a Dutch artist in his studio, seated before his easel and contemplating a model in contemporary clothing who, with her crown of laurel, her trumpet, and her volume of Thucydides, in fact is identifiable as Clio, the muse of History. The sense of a staged performance is further underlined by the enormous curtain at the left that, as if in front of a theater proscenium, suddenly discloses a tableau vivant. Having paid homage to this masterpiece by meticulously cloning every square inch of Vermeer's canvas, Deem then goes on to recreate it again, but this time after the painting has voyaged for three centuries across the Atlantic, miraculously landing in New York in the studio of a contemporary artist. It is only slowly that we observe all the changes in time and space. The clothing, of course, is most pronouncedly different, although the backs of both artists are covered with a similarly striped pattern. But more subtly, Vermeer's wall tapestry, a map of the United Netherlands, has become a map of the United States (extending the George Washington metaphor), and the town views on the borders of the Dutch map have similarly been Americanized. Moreover, the twentieth-century world has crept in stealthily, not only in the way that Vermeer's elaborate chandelier has been replaced by a utilitarian ceiling lamp, but by the subtly surprising transformation of the allegorical trumpet into a telephone and the appearance of a small TV set in lieu of the weighty book Vermeer

placed behind the curtain. And even the curtain, we eventually notice, is no longer made of a lush fabric with an intricate floral design, but offers instead a theatrical swag made of American patchwork-quilt patterns.

Vermeer's interiors are so real to Deem that, like a stage director or a modern resident, he can enter them and rearrange them at will. So it is that these 1970s variations on Vermeer's *Music Lesson* and *The Artist in His Studio (An Allegory of History)* continue to live and breathe two decades later. In the 1998 *Vermeer's "Music Lesson" with the Figures Removed* (see p. 76), not only have the music-making lady and her male friend vanished, but so have the carpet-covered table and still life in the right foreground. Moreover, the portrait of George Washington over the virginal has been replaced by the mirror from Vermeer's original painting, except, of course, that it now has no one to reflect, and can only offer us an angled view of the checkerboard floor. As a subliminal echo of the pair of figures in the Vermeer, Deem then adds a second chair against the wall, almost as if, in his mind's eye, he had for the moment snuck out of this Vermeer to get a chair from another one.

In the 1999 *Vermeer's Easel* (see p. 77), the same wizardry reigns. Again, the scene has been deserted by its former occupants, the artist and his allegorical model, leaving as interior furnishings nothing but the map of the Netherlands, the chandelier, an empty easel, two chairs, and a stool. And at times, these interiors can be pared down to only one piece of furniture, as in the 2003 *Vermeer Detail* (see p. 61), where we see nothing but a precious fragment of a painting by Vermeer, a wooden stool presented against a blank wall and a checkerboard floor as if it were a holy relic from a lost treasure or perhaps the lone survivor from an antique dollhouse. The enchantment of old-master realist painting – to make us feel that, miraculously, the canvas permits us to peer into a seamless fusion of our own reality with that invented by the painter – has rarely been embraced so fully. We feel that Deem, whether awake or asleep, lives in Vermeer's spaces, sitting on his chairs, listening to his music, looking out of his glazed windows, basking in his suffused light.

To be sure, Vermeer has remained Deem's life-long obsession, abundantly represented in every decade of his work. But as this encyclopedic anthology makes clear, this is only one part of his story which now, in retrospect, can be seen more clearly as playing a large and often precocious role in the new viewpoints that emerged in the 1960s and then, in the hands of younger generations, continued to flourish. It is worth looking back to 1963, the year of Deem's first one-man show at the Allan Stone Gallery, New York, where, together with variations on Raeburn, Vermeer, and Alma-Tadema, he exhibited other old-master quotations from the same vintage: *Double Dutch Landscape* (see p. 55), *Multiple Frans Hals* (p. 48), and *Composition with Millet* (p. 33). All of these join forces with contemporary art-world events. The grid of six black-and-white reproductions of Hals's famous witch of Haarlem, *Malle Babba*, each slightly different from its neighbor, is a perfect old-master pendant to Warhol's

Marilyns and Mona Lisas. Such a grid format, in fact, kept cropping up in his work, as in the *November 1966 Calendar*, with its Jasper Johns-like alterations to the numerical sequence (p. 101); the 1983 encyclopedic portrait gallery of all the presidents of the United States in a pattern of eight-times-nine squares that end with Reagan in mid-presidency and leave nine squares blank for the future (p. 100); or the 2002 *Bruegel Tiles* (pp. 38–39), which offers six-times-four ceramic squares, each slightly weathered and each depicting a single figure excerpted from the old master's repertory. As for the reproductions of Millet's *Man with a Hoe* on one canvas and the twin Dutch landscapes by Hobbema and Ruisdael on another, these add another component that connects with Deem's contemporaries, namely, calligraphy. In both works, the bare white background on which the painted reproductions hover is marked by what looks like an inscription from a precious manuscript, a gossamer tangle of words that, in fact, proves to be illegible. The connections to the art of the 1950s become clearer when we remember that earlier, in 1959, Deem had painted *A Letter to Mark Tobey* (see p. 91), a large canvas composed of nothing but line after line of the most elegant, yet undecipherable handwriting, an homage to the older master whose own vocabulary was based on just this kind of abstract calligraphy. And looking elsewhere in the decade, this attraction to making paintings and drawings, both legible and illegible, from what looks like written evidence that has survived from another century, is also shared by Cy Twombly.

If Deem, as a young artist, could imagine writing a letter to his twentieth-century senior, Mark Tobey, these leaps of fantasy within art history's museum-without-walls kept proliferating. Hobbema's famous tree-lined road, already used in 1963, could reappear in 1971 as a perspectival mirage viewed through a windshield in a car whose rear-view mirror reflects the bespectacled eyes of the artist himself at the wheel of this dream voyage into seventeenth-century Holland (see p. 54). Moreover, artists' ghosts can be retrieved through their own paintings. In 1995, Deem reincarnated a 1959 painting by Edward Hopper, *Excursion into Philosophy*, that presented an open volume of Plato on a plain cot where the disconnected intimacy of an anonymous couple is revealed. The man is seated, the woman is lying down, her back to him, her buttocks exposed. But in Deem's version, the pair is transformed into Hopper himself, seated beside his wife Jo, accompanied by the same volume of Plato and the same glowing rectangles of yellow, window-framed sunlight (see p. 99). And earlier, in 1989, he performed a similar feat of spiritualism, now conjuring up the three-dimensional specters of the young Arshile Gorky and his dead mother, who have materialized from the treasured old photograph from Armenia that, decades later in New York, Gorky had used to trigger his memory of a heart-breaking family history and to paint the canvas now placed by Deem on an easel in a room haunted by memories of the Old World (see p. 112).

Deem's free-flowing fantasies about the facts and the fictions of art history take many forms, among which is the matter-of-fact but totally unimaginable painting of 1980, *Auction* (see pp. 30–31), in which we get an oblique glimpse of the usual business going on at Sotheby's or Christie's, except for the fact that all of the pictures on the walls that are up for sale to this prosaic, contemporary audience of buyers are renowned, from Velázquez, Hobbema and Rubens to Cabanel, Remington and Picasso, with a precious Vermeer, the *Girl with a Pearl Earring*, just about to go on the block. Similarly, the holdings of the Musée d'Orsay can come to life in unexpected ways in a painting of 1997, in which decadent Romans, Parisian musicians and floorscrapers, and Courbet himself all come to life in a new community populated only by excerpts from painted fictions (see p. 21). Such adventures in art-historical time and space are common in Deem's work, but they reach maximum complexity in an ongoing series with the title "School of…" These schools of famous artists and styles – Raphael, Caravaggio, Velázquez, Rembrandt, Ingres, Gauguin, Cubism, Art Deco, Bauhaus and more – spring from Deem's own childhood memories going back to before the Second World War, when he attended a simple, rural school in his hometown, Vincennes, Indiana. It was this schoolroom itself, with its regular grid of plain, wooden desks framed by the equally strict rectangular patterns of windows and blackboards, that not only served as the site of enchantment, but also provided a prophecy of the spare and perfect geometries that would mesmerize Deem in Vermeer's interior designs. In this bare chamber of his boyhood memories, the artist could go on to imagine all of art history paying brief visits and then, with a magic thunderclap, disappearing. Already in 1979, Deem painted with his usual precision of detail a sharp-focus recall of this schoolroom emptied of students and teacher (see pp. 104–5), the only presences being the American flag and two paintings, the Stuart portrait of Washington and a Frederick Remington, both of which would make later appearances in his work. And the schoolroom itself could stretch and change in later imagination, as in *Everybody's Schoolroom* of 1994 (see pp. 108–9), where the grid of desks expands to factory numbers, the Washington portrait on the wall turns into an Alma-Tadema print, and the framed windows become floating voids through which the shifting clouds and landscape outside begin to penetrate this disciplined world. But mainly, it is art history that wafts into this treasured memory of the childhood room in which dreams could come and go. In *Hudson River School* of 1995 (see p. 94), the grid of desks is unexpectedly moved outdoors, half-sheltered on a rounded balcony that now locates the school in Olana, Frederick Church's lavish dream house, and offers the absent students the kind of Hudson River view that inspired Church and his contemporaries. In *School of Velázquez* of 1987 (see p. 26), it is *Las Meninas* that triggers the apparition in the schoolroom, with the desks in one-point perspective merging uninterrupted with the rectangular spaces of Velázquez's vast room, whose insistent rectangular frames recall both the austere, perpendicular patterns in the schoolroom interior and those on the floors and walls of

Vermeer's domestic spaces. In *The Spanish School* of 1993 (see p. 35), Velázquez is replaced by his contemporaries who specialized in *bodegones* (still lifes), masters like Zurbarán and Sanchez Cotán whose hyper-realist still-life objects – lemons, pitchers, flowers, cups – are removed from their table-tops and now placed on the schoolroom desktops in tandem with the open books of childhood memory. In *The Studio of Jacques-Louis David* of 1996 (see p. 23), the history of French painting seems to float through a painting in the Louvre by Léon-Matthieu Cochereau that recorded the master's zealous students working from a nude academic model. This, too, is rendered in one-point perspective. Now, however, David's studio is populated by figures culled from his own paintings, as well as from those of his predecessors and heirs (Lépicié, Corot, Degas) and even from a transatlantic portrait by Gilbert Stuart. Elsewhere, sex materializes from classroom daydreams. In the *School of Modigliani* of 1988 (see p. 119), one of the painter's voluptuous supine nudes drops from the sky onto a desktop, while two of the artist's primmer, more fully clothed figures take their places as vigilant schoolmaster and schoolmistress.

These art-historical reveries continue right into the more adventurous territory of what for post-modern decades has become the heroic, early years of "modern art." *Cubist Cache* of 1995 (see pp. 110–11) is crammed with still-life quotations cut out like collages from famous works in the Cubist pantheon, their flattened planes precariously jostling for place on the impossibly tilted floorboards of Caillebotte's *Floorscrapers* (one of Deem's favorite perspectival references) and including, as a surprise, a neo-Picassoid chair by David Hockney, whose nostalgic vision of Picasso and early modernism parallels Deem's own variations on the long-ago rebels who, to everybody's surprise, became museum-worthy masters. It is a glimpse back to the grand, innovative moments of the last century that is also found in *Bauhaus School* of 1986 (see p. 120), where the ghosts of the Bauhaus masters themselves line up in front of a machine-age version of the rural desktops from Deem's childhood, now drawn with the precision of a modern architect's ruler and compass, and now fused with Schlemmer's signature painting of the Bauhaus staircase. Through the giant windows, we see a view of Gropius's Brave New World architecture, now as distant from the present as the Indiana landscape outside the schoolhouse window.

It goes without saying that Deem's immaculately crafted retrospections, with their mixture of personal history and art history, are a singular achievement; yet enduring artists don't work in a vacuum but reflect those aspects of the changing world they live in that will also be mirrored in the art of their contemporaries. Deem is no exception. His private vision, in fact, coincides again and again with what older and younger generations of artists, not to mention architects, were thinking and making during the last four decades, when contemporary art began to look backwards as much as forwards and when the nineteenth century's passion for historical revival,

once scorned by modernists, was itself revived. Already in the 1960s, Deem introduced the replication of old-master reproductions, often parallelling Warhol's embrace of the photographic image; and by the 1970s, he had already mastered the technique of replicating old-master paintings themselves, scrupulously cloning, in particular, the miraculous illusions and surfaces of Vermeer. And his trip through the looking glass of painting also permitted him to wander freely about the alternative realities he found in the old masters' painted time capsules, from whose borrowed parts he made startlingly unfamiliar wholes. Looking at the work of younger artists from the late twentieth century, it is amazing to see how often Deem prophesies their concerns. As for his narrative recreations from the venerable pages of art history, here are previews of Mark Tansey's Vasari-like illustrations to great moments imagined from the same annals. As for his painstaking cloning of famous paintings, begun in the early 1960s, these too look forward to Elaine Sturtevant, an artist of his generation who, in the same decade, began to replicate the work of the artist-stars of the 1960s (Johns, Stella, Warhol, etc.) as well as many artists who emerged in the 1980s, such as Mike Bidlo and Richard Pettibone. And not least, his imaginative rambling through the stage sets and players of the old masters, using them for new dramas and comedies, prefigures the work of many painters who also want to reanimate the encyclopedia of art history whose images, repeated *ad infinitum*, have long ago lost their original luster. Among these artists are Russell

Connor, who joins quotations from disparate paintings with often hilarious results; Kathleen Gilje, who, with amazing craftsmanship, replicates old-master paintings but gives them one comic twist; Sophie Matisse, who, as Deem had so often done with Vermeer, depopulates famous paintings, leaving us the setting without the people; Sandow Birk, who recreates Hudson River landscape paintings, but adds nineteenth-century penitentiaries to these Gardens of Eden. And in photography, too, there are the examples of Cindy Sherman and Yasumasa Morimura, who stage tableaux vivants of old-master paintings but turn the faces into self-portraits. The list, in fact, keeps swelling, a sure sign that the work of George Deem, for all its seeming uniqueness and eccentricity, helped lay the very foundations of "the art of art history."

School of Rembrandt, 1989

PREFACE

In my work, quoting pictures by other artists, I make paintings of paintings, new works from existing works. I call attention to my use of known images when I quote such familiar pictures as the *Mona Lisa*, Gilbert Stuart's unfinished portrait of George Washington, Vermeer's *Girl with a Pearl Earring*, and Manet's picnic scene, *Le Déjeuner sur l'herbe*. Like a flag or a pyramid, a cross or the shape of a key, these images are recognizable in an unexpected context and even when altered, as in my George Washington paintings and drawings.

We do not have to make repeated visits to the Louvre for the *Mona Lisa* to become imprinted in

our consciousness. That comes about willy-nilly from constantly seeing reproductions. We go to the Louvre to compare the actual painting by Leonardo with our mental image of it. Even if seeing the original for the first time, we cannot help but see it as one image in a series. It is too late to look at the *Mona Lisa* with virgin eyes.

The same thing is true in music. You have already heard Beethoven's Fifth Symphony before you listen to it for the first time. In his "1812 Overture" Tchaikovsky quoted the French national anthem "La Marseillaise" with the certainty that you would recognize the quotation. Quotation famously was a method of composition for the American composer Charles Ives, who made new music of other people's music: Beethoven, Tchaikovsky, American Protestant hymns, popular tunes, marches, and patriotic songs ("My Old Kentucky Home," "Yankee Doodle," "My Country 'Tis of Thee," "America the Beautiful"). The contemporary American composer David Borden incorporates a solo violin part from Mozart's Violin Concerto No. 3 in G Major into his electronic score *K216.01* composed in 2003 ("K216" is the number assigned to this violin concerto in the Koechel Catalogue of the works of Mozart). Borden's title *K216.01* indicates his quoted source, artist and work.

Vermeer's "Lady Seated at a Virginal,"
the Lady Removed, 1999

The number "01" suggests future additions to the series initiated by Mozart and extended by Borden.

It is not in a spirit of competition that Charles Ives quotes Beethoven and Tchaikovsky, David Borden quotes Mozart, and I quote Gilbert Stuart and Leonardo da Vinci. Music and painting are not competitive sports. In a footnote to one of his songs, Charles Ives wrote,

Neither Schumann, Brahms, nor Franz
will be the one to suffer by a comparison.
… Moreover, they would probably be
the last to claim a monopoly of anything –
especially the right of man to the
pleasure of trying to express in
music whatever he wants to.

When he quotes unaltered the solo violin part from Mozart's violin concerto in his composition *K216.01*, David Borden parallels my practice in my 1979 two-canvas work *New York Artist in His Studio/ Vermeer's "Artist in His Studio"* (see pp. 64–65). The canvas on the right is a same-size copy of Vermeer's painting *The Artist in His Studio* (1666–67). The canvas on the left depicts, in the same format, a New York artist in *his* studio. That canvas is painted from life. The studio is an actual loft space in New York. I am the artist seated before an easel. A model posed for me, holding a telephone and the New York yellow pages telephone directory. The video monitor on the table suggests how a painter might be enabled to paint his own back and include himself in his painting.

Many artists have learned by making copies of the paintings of earlier artists. When I quote the painting of another artist, however much I may learn in doing so, I have another purpose. Like the composers Charles Ives and David Borden, I integrate the quoted work into a new composition with its own design and structure and inherent meaning. That meaning includes the recognition that every painting has in it the possibility of another painting.

THE HISTORY OF ART

A painter's history of art is in my case a history of painting. Not a history of all painting from prehistoric caves on, but Western painting as it has been practiced since the fifteenth century in Europe, and wherever migrating Europeans have carried the tradition with them. Western painting has two distinguishing characteristics. One is the use of oil paint as a medium. The other is the use of perspective to render an effect of three-dimensional depth on a painting's two-dimensional flat surface. This is the tradition of painting that I am involved with.

My engagement with various aspects of Western painting suggested the chapter divisions. This chapter begins appropriately near the beginning of Western painting with my response to Raphael's canonical *School of Athens* (opposite). Raphael's picture in one-point perspective is a wall painting in fresco. My *School of Athens* is painted in oil on canvas. A painting on canvas is a portable object. Among other things that can be done with it, it can be bought and sold. The final image in this chapter is *Auction* (pp. 30–31).

School of Athens, 1998 (opposite)
The School of Athens (1509–11) is a fresco painting by Raphael on the wall of a room in the Vatican. Philosophy is Raphael's theme; the figures exemplify various schools of thought within the Western tradition. At the center are Plato and Aristotle, standing side by side in an imaginary architectural setting expressive of High Renaissance ideals of scale, magnificence, and harmony. Raphael – shifting metaphorical levels – punctuates his scene with such schoolroom props as books and slates and globes. In my *School of Athens*, I introduced the furniture of the schoolroom, desks lined up in rows facing the teacher.

The Triumph of Art, 1990 (pp. 18–19)
The Triumph of Art derives from Mantegna's *The Triumphs of Caesar* (1486–93), a series of paintings in which Mantegna imaginatively recreated the parade given to a victorious Roman general upon his return to Rome. In my painting the parade is passing in front of the Guggenheim Museum on Fifth Avenue – New York is the scene of the Triumph of Art. The captured treasures include a still life of flowers by Cézanne, Vermeer's *Milkmaid*, Edward Hopper's *Early Sunday Morning*, Thomas Eakins's *Max Schmitt in a Single Scull*, the *Mona Lisa*, paintings by Matisse, Jim Dine, and Frank Stella, a sculpture of a female nude by Gaston Lachaise, and a Roman bust of the goddess Venus.

L'Ecole des Beaux-Arts, 1991 (below)
Le Musée d'Orsay, 1997 (opposite)

Le Musée d'Orsay listens in on the unending conversation of pictures with other pictures through time. I quote four key works from this Paris museum's collection of nineteenth-century French paintings. Couture's *Romans of the Decadence* (1847) borrows from Raphael and Veronese to make a challenging statement of faith in the long tradition of painting. Courbet responds to that statement with another epic painting, *The Painter's Studio* (1855), which he combatively subtitled "A Real Allegory." His painting is populated with the figures of "real" people, the contemporary artists and writers who were part of his circle. Courbet has positioned himself at the center of his painting in a self-portrait of the painter seated before his easel. I have quoted Courbet's central group of figures: the seated artist, his model, and the boy standing at the artist's knee. The group of musicians is from *The Orchestra of the Opera* (1868) by Degas. I have removed the stage and orchestra pit in his painting to make way for the floorboards in Caillebotte's *Floorscrapers* (1875). The floorboards are lit from the columned atrium of *The Romans of the Decadence*, and I have added the figure of a fourth floorscraper. The point where Courbet's paint-laden brush touches the canvas on his easel is the exact center of my composition in which one may see Couture behind Courbet, and Courbet through Caillebotte and Degas.

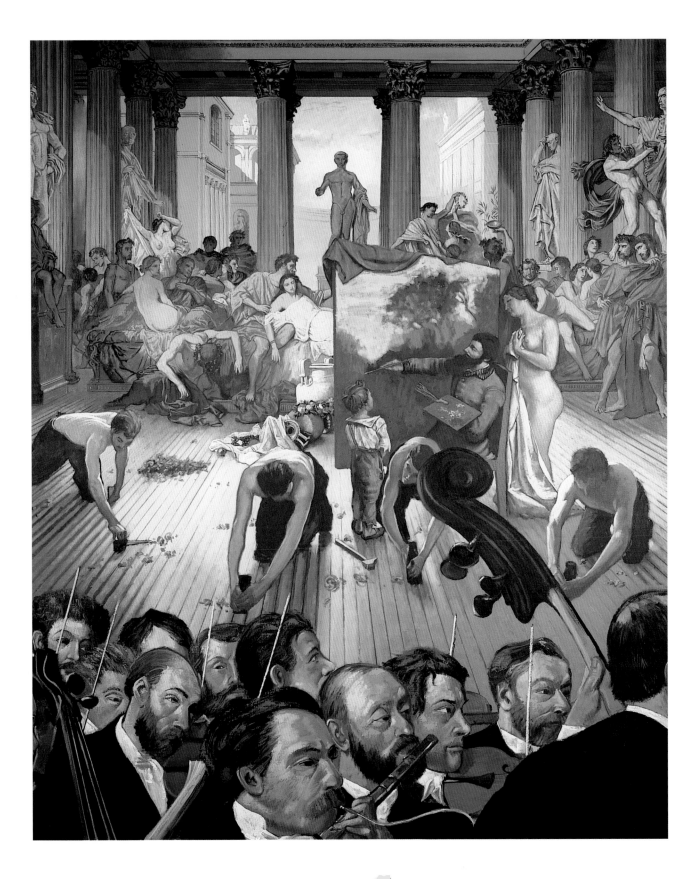

Del Sarto Canaletto Titian, 1995 (above)

Del Sarto Canaletto Titian quotes three paintings in the collection of the National Gallery in London. Andrea del Sarto's *Portrait of a Young Man* (1517) and Titian's *Portrait of a Man* (1512) are mirror images of each other. When I put the two figures back to back in an oil study on paper, I liked the resulting image – the battle of the sleeves, the eyes following the viewer. But I preferred a vertical composition that would retain the format of a portrait. A third painting in the National Gallery's collection gave me my unifying image: *Venice: Piazza San Marco* (after 1756) by Canaletto. I also enjoyed the art-historical pleasantry of moving the Florentine painter Del Sarto to Venice for his meeting with the Venetian master Titian.

The sitter in Titian's *Portrait of a Man* rests his arm on a stone ledge, a parapet which defines the picture plane and locates the figure behind it. I have replaced Titian's stone ledge with a wood sill into which are carved the names of the three painters whose works I have quoted: DEL SARTO CANALETTO TITIAN.

The Studio of Jacques-Louis David, 1996 (opposite)

Boston Pastime, 1988

Easel Painting, 1993 (right)

The traditional branches of painting
come together in *Easel Painting* (1993) –
self-portrait, portrait, interior, still life,
and landscape. This painting uses a
technique of self-quotation. Each image
has its source in an earlier painting by
me. See *The Landscape Painter* (p. 28),
and *Portrait on Demand* (p. 98).

School of Velázquez, 1987 (opposite)

The Landscape Painter, 1993
The artist's studio in *The Landscape Painter*
is illuminated from a single light source
emanating from the landscape which I have
painted on a table as if it were a still-life
arrangement.

Auction, 1980

EUROPEAN PAINTING

In *Sebastian in the Kitchen* (see pp. 50–51) one sees a nearly nude young man standing behind a woman pouring milk from a pitcher into a bowl. From the title of the painting, we know that the young man is named Sebastian. We do not know who Sebastian is, nor what brings him and the woman together in what may be assumed to be her kitchen. The image prompts questions. Does she know that he is there? Does he know where he is? Is she determined to ignore him and get on with what she appears to be so intent on doing?

Although the pictures tell their own story to the eye, much of European painting also includes a literary narrative of stories from Greek and Roman mythology, the Bible, and ancient and European history. These paintings were made for people who already knew the story, and understood the visual codes and symbols that identified gods and goddesses, heroes, and saints. A standing male nude figure, his body pierced with arrows, signified Saint Sebastian in whatever setting the figure was placed. The Sebastian in the kitchen in my painting is Antonello da Messina's *Saint Sebastian* (*c.* 1475–77). The kitchen belongs to Vermeer's *Milkmaid* (*c.* 1658–60). I include Vermeer's kitchen window, rug-covered table, and other objects as identifying visual attributes of the figure of the Milkmaid. This is the Milkmaid, always, anywhere (*Vermeer Palette*, see pp. 58–59). Each visual quotation of the figure of the Milkmaid inescapably is a reference to Vermeer's painting *The Milkmaid* and adds to the painting's iconographic significance. In my painting, I quote two iconic paintings, Vermeer's and Antonello's. We do not have to look beyond painting itself for our gods and goddesses, our heroes and saints.

Composition with Millet, 1963 (opposite)

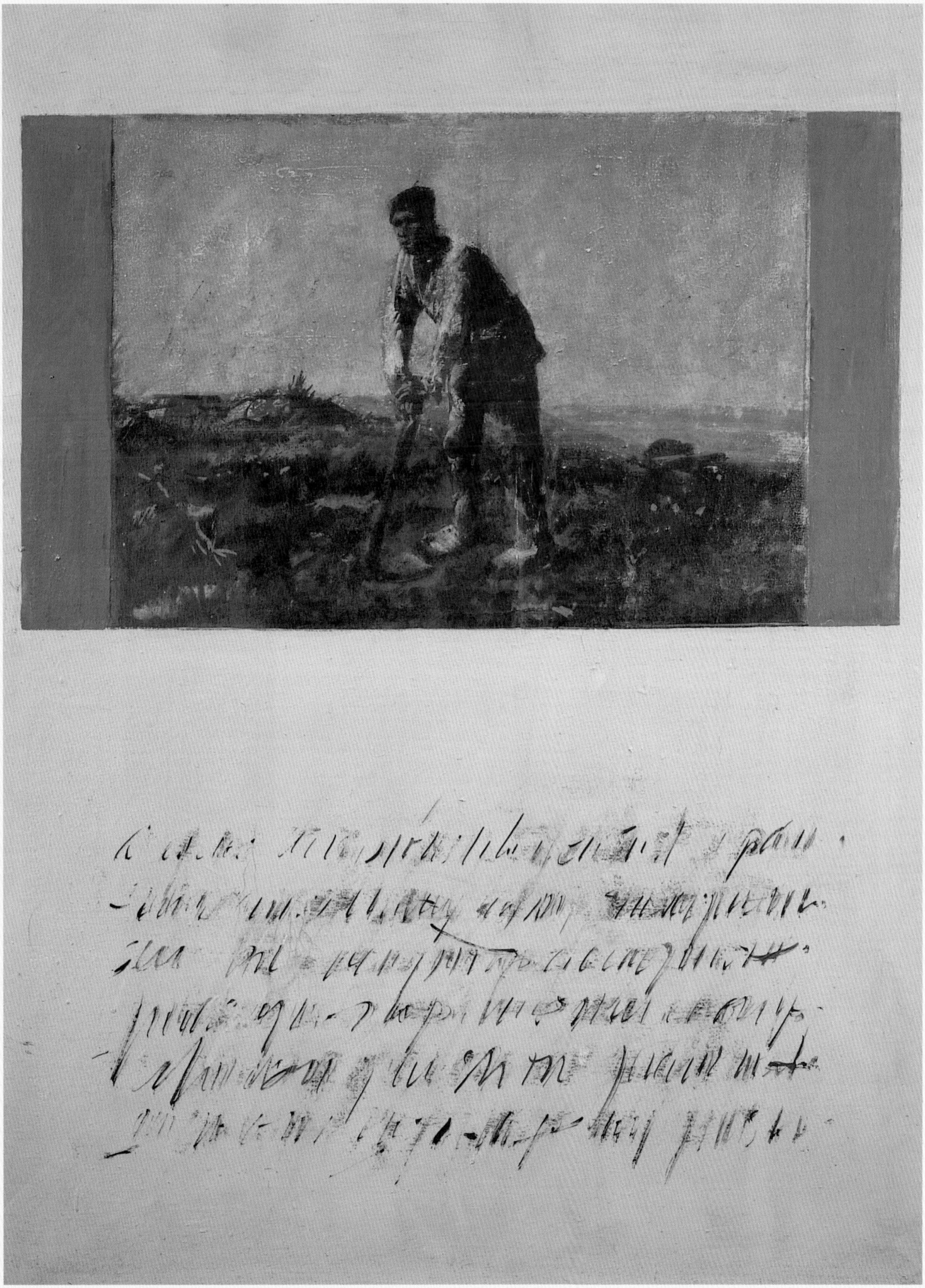

School of Caravaggio, 1984

The Spanish School, 1993

Terborch Silver Dresses, 1979 (below)

The Caravaggio Saint Matthew, 1979 (opposite)
Red, yellow, and blue, *The Caravaggio Saint Matthew* is a baroque theatrical riff on three paintings by Caravaggio (1571–1610) in the Church of San Luigi dei Francesi in Rome. In them Caravaggio depicts three episodes in the story of Saint Matthew: the calling of Matthew by Christ to become a disciple,

Matthew writing his Gospel of Christ's life and teachings, and the Saint's martyrdom. I have quoted Caravaggio's paintings in their entirety at the bottom of my painting as color-coded footnotes to my composition. The fourth footnote painting shows the façade of the Church of San Luigi dei Francesi.

Bruegel Tiles, 2002

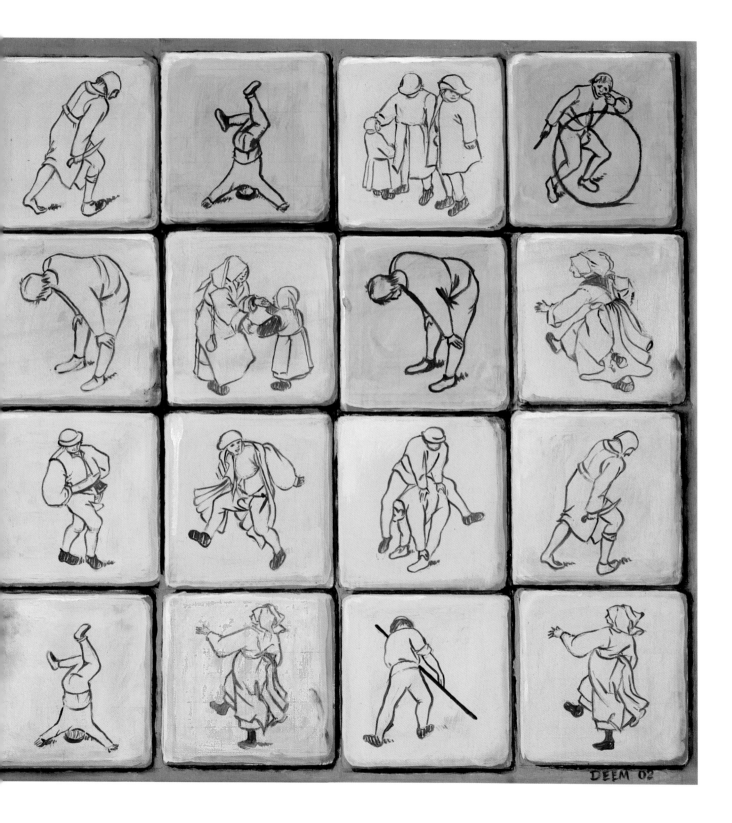

Ellen and George, 1983 (above)

Portrait of Mary Ellen Andrews in a Renaissance Landscape, 1972 (opposite)

DEEM '71

An English Quilt, 1971 (above)

An English Painting, 1965 (right)

42

43

Occidental Rug, 1970 (above)
Composition With Women, 1966 (opposite)

School of Courbet, 1988

Multiple Frans Hals, 1963 (opposite)

Composition in Red and Black, 1972 (below)

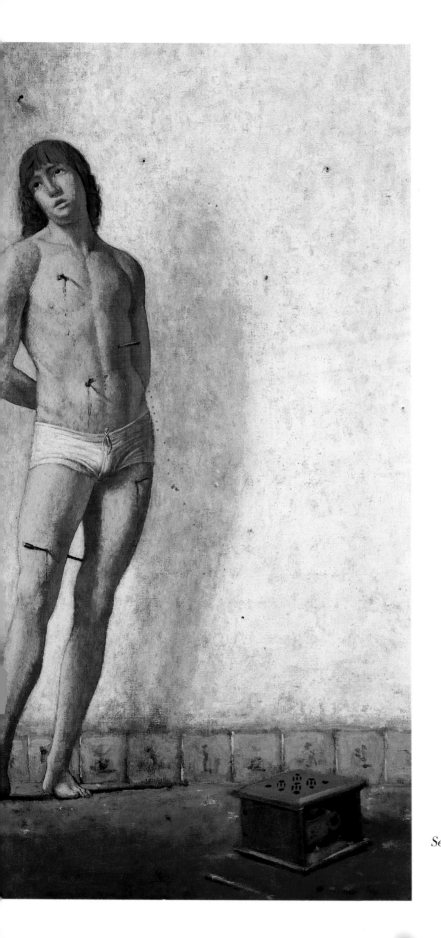

Sebastian in the Kitchen, 1977

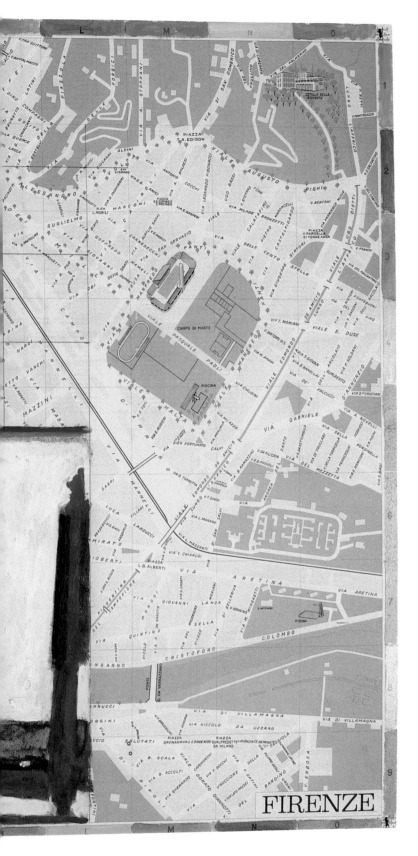

Vermeer in Florence, 1976

Auto Portrait, 1971 (left)

The road is in a Dutch landscape painting by Hobbema (1638–1709). The face is mine, painted as if reflected in a mirror the same shape and size as the rearview mirror in my 1962 Volkswagen car.

Double Dutch Landscape, 1963 (below)

HOW TO PAINT A VERMEER

Vermeer was born in Delft in 1632 and died there forty-three years later in 1675. He painted two to three pictures a year, selling them to private clients in Delft. One collector, Pieter van Ruijven, who became a lifelong friend, appears to have bought a painting every year, acquiring close to half of Vermeer's production. The documentary evidence of Vermeer's rate of production is confirmed by the paintings themselves: they are too patiently rendered for them to have been turned out rapidly. We can be sure from the perfect finish of his paintings that time meant nothing to Vermeer. He painted not to get it done, but to get it right.

In Vermeer's pictures almost nothing is happening. A woman reads a letter, a woman writes a letter, a woman tries on a pearl necklace, a woman opens a casement window, a woman pours milk from a jug. What movement there is, is stilled. The figures are poised in a contemplative silence. It is a marvelous fact that each time I look at one of these deceptively simple paintings I see something in it that I have not seen before. That, of course, is in part because I have changed in the interim. It is like the experience of re-reading a novel. The novel cannot mean to us what it did when we first read it because we have changed so much in our understanding of things. And the fact of our having read the novel alters our response to it the second time round. We now know its structure and how it will end. When I respond to a painting by Vermeer with a painting of my own, my painting changes how I see the Vermeer. Again, think of a novel. I change the ending. I then see something in the Vermeer that I had not seen before. My response is to make a new painting. That is how to paint a Vermeer.

Deem Vermeer, 1974 (opposite)

Vermeer Palette, 1983

A Stool, a Chair, and a Map, 2003 (opposite)
Vermeer Detail, 2003 (below)

The Art of Painting, 2002, diptych

Following pages (pp. 64–65):
New York Artist in His Studio/Vermeer's "Artist in His Studio," 1979, diptych

Seven Vermeer Corners, 1999

An American Vermeer, 1970–71

Vermeer's Red Rug, 1981 (above)

Study for Vermeer's "Concert"
with Two Figures Removed, 1997 (opposite)

How to Paint a Vermeer, 1981

The Red Chair, 2002 (above)
Painting Perspective, 2001 (right)

Vermeer's "Music Lesson" with the Figures Removed, 1998 (above)

Vermeer's Easel, 1999 (right)

Extended Vermeer, 2000 (opposite)
Woman with a Water Pitcher, 2002 (right)

Vermeer Interior without Figure, 1970 (opposite)

Vermeer's Chair, 1994 (below)

AMERICAN PAINTING

During the Colonial Period American painters looked to the mother country for example and instruction. Gilbert Stuart (1755–1828), born in Rhode Island, learned his trade in London as a studio assistant to the Pennsylvania-born painter Benjamin West (1738–1820). West, who became the second President of the Royal Academy, remained in England after the end of the Revolutionary War. Gilbert Stuart returned home to paint portraits of the prominent citizens of the new Republic, including 114 portraits of George Washington. Only three of Stuart's portraits of Washington were painted from life. The rest are replicas. See *George Washington and His Portrait* (opposite), and my quotations of English portrait painting, *An English Quilt* (p. 42) and *An English Painting* (p. 43).

American painters throughout the nineteenth century studied in Europe. Philadelphia-born Thomas Eakins (1844–1916) studied in Paris and Spain, returning home to become a teacher at the Pennsylvania Academy of Fine Arts. His pictures were informed by the breadth and depth of his interest in science, medicine, anatomy, motion, and perspective. See *Eakins and Apples*, page 95.

Technical training was hard to come by for an American painter like George Caleb Bingham (1811–79) who stayed at home. Before embarking at age 21 on a career as a portrait painter in his native Missouri, Bingham learned cabinet-making and sign-painting. *Bingham Ceiling* (p. 93), with a nod to the cabinet-maker, quotes Bingham's emblematic paintings of American life in the young Republic.

There was no need for Americans to go abroad to become painters by the time I arrived in New York in 1958. Everything was here. Bingham had suffered from the lack of paintings to look at. I find no end to the paintings to be seen in New York. And no end to the cascading flow of visual information from advertising and corporate images and signs and logos (*American Express*, p. 88, *Random House*, p. 89). *An American Rug* (p. 92) brings together a still-life painting by Chardin (1699–1779), a magazine covergirl illustration, and Bingham's *Raftsmen Playing Cards* (1847).

George Washington and His Portrait, 1972 (opposite) – caption overleaf

George Washington and His Portrait,
1972 (see p. 83)
The source is Gilbert Stuart's 1797
portrait of George Washington, now in
the Huntington Library Art Collection
in San Marino, California. I followed
Stuart's paint application and color for
the "portrait" in my painting. But when
painting the foreground image of George
Washington seen in front of his portrait,
his shadow falling upon the painting behind
him, I dulled Stuart's color, using a gray
glaze to produce the appearance of a
photographic studio portrait.

George Washington in White Face, 1974 (above)
George Washington Shaving, 1992 (opposite)

Mona Lisa Washington, 1972 (right)

George Washington Vermeer, 1974 (opposite)

In *George Washington Vermeer*, I quote two paintings:
Vermeer's *Music Lesson* (1662–65) and Gilbert Stuart's unfinished
portrait of George Washington (1796). I removed Vermeer's
two standing figures of a woman and a man, and replaced
Vermeer's mirror on the wall above the virginal with the
portrait of George Washington. My black and brown and white
palette alludes to the black-and-white image of Washington
on the American dollar bill (the greenback is printed in green
ink on the back only). Also, I like the analogy to the black-
and-white crispness of historical documents displayed as
objects for observation.

Random House, 1975 (above)

American Express, 2000 (opposite)

Ruscha, 2001 (above)
A Letter to Mark Tobey, 1959 (opposite)

An American Rug, 1970 (above)
Bingham Ceiling, 1993 (opposite)

Hudson River School, 1995 (below)

The view of the Hudson River in my *Hudson River School* (1995)
is the view from Olana, the house built in the 1870s by the painter
Frederick Edwin Church (1826–1900) on a hill near the town of
Hudson, New York. And it is the scene Walt Whitman imagined
in his poem "When Lilacs Last in the Dooryard Bloom'd:"

…at sundown, and the gray smoke lucid and bright,
With floods of the yellow gold of the gorgeous, indolent,
   sinking sun, burning, expanding the air…
In the distance the flowing glaze, the breast of the river…

Eakins and Apples, 1981 (above)

A Painting for Babies, 1970/1980 (above)
MacDowell Colony, 1978 (opposite)

Portrait on Demand, 1992 (above)
Is the gunman a model holding a pose as
instructed by the artist? Or is the artist
producing a portrait at gunpoint?

Edward and Jo Hopper, 1995

G. WASHINGTON   J. ADAMS   T. JEFFERSON   J. MADISON   J. MONROE

J. Q. ADAMS   A. JACKSON   M. VAN BUREN   W. H. HARRISON

J. TYLER   J. K. POLK   Z. TAYLOR   M. FILLMORE   F. PIERCE

J. BUCHANAN   A. LINCOLN   A. JOHNSON   U. S. GRANT   R. B. HAYES

J. GARFIELD   C. ARTHUR   G. CLEVELAND   B. HARRISON   G. CLEVELAND   W. McKINLEY

T. ROOSEVELT   W. TAFT   W. WILSON   W. HARDING

C. COOLIDGE   H. HOOVER   F. D. ROOSEVELT   H. S. TRUMAN

D. EISENHOWER   J. F. KENNEDY   L. B. JOHNSON   R. NIXON

G. FORD   J. CARTER   R. REAGAN

November Calendar, 1966 (above)

The Presidents of the United States, 1983 (opposite)

Ashcan School, 1987

The Fall of Whistler's Mother, 1969

Schoolroom, 1979

MODERNISM

It is useful to distinguish between *modern* and *modernism*. Ours is the Modern period of history after the Middle Ages, from the fifteenth century to the present day. *Modern* implies a break with what has gone before. Western painting was born with the modern world. *Modern* also means what is in fashion and up-to-date, as opposed to what is old-fashioned and out-of-date. This meaning is associated particularly with the succession of avant-garde art movements that followed one another from about 1850 to about 1960: Realism, Impressionism, Post-Impressionism, Cubism, Surrealism, etc. This was modernism.

Modernist artists conspicuously departed from the forms and conventions of the art that had gone before them. Their rupture with the past was widely viewed as a revolutionary rejection of the values of Western art. It was thought that the new broom of modernism was sweeping earlier painting styles out of present relevance into the dustbin of history. In with the new! Out with the old! As modernism passes into history, other considerations come into play. Were modernist artists – like the revolutionary Russian poet Mayakovsky – engaged in the demolition of Western painting (*Mayakovsky in Delft*, see p. 123)? Or is modernism one style among others within the Western tradition (*Hans Hofmann Vermeer*, opposite)?

Hans Hofmann Vermeer, 1980

Everybody's Schoolroom, 1994

Cubist Cache, 1995

What does Paris do with its Cubist art in August? When the Parisians are away on their summer vacations they store their cubist art in a room that Caillebotte's floorscrapers have left vacant (*Le Musée d'Orsay*, see p. 21). The cubist objects in *Cubist Cache* are none of them sculptures. They are cubist paintings by Picasso, Braque, Malevich, David Hockney, Juan Gris, and Le Corbusier. David Hockney's *Chair* (1985), when repeated smaller scale to the right of the table, flanks Picasso's *Skull and Pitcher* (1945). The grouping of guitar and bottles on the floor at the base of the painting is quoted from Le Corbusier's *Still Life* (1920). The black pears to the right are from *Pears and Grapes on a Table* (1913) by Juan Gris.

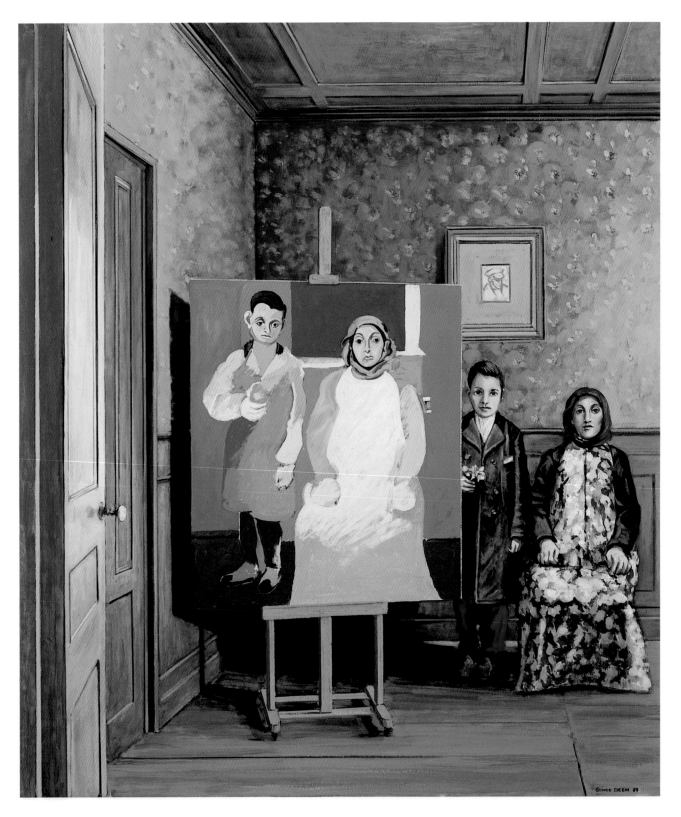

Arshile Gorky and His Mother, 1989 (opposite)

School of Arshile Gorky, 1995 (below)
It is perhaps the first day of school. Flowers in hand, the
young painter-to-be Arshile Gorky has arrived with his mother.
The picture on the wall behind them is my reduction of *The Sacred
Grove* (1884–89), a painting by Puvis de Chavannes who when
he died in 1898 was the most famous painter in France. Seurat,
Gauguin, and Matisse all responded to the decorative flatness,
the airless tranquility in his clearly delineated compositions.

Manet Palette, 1994 (above)

A Working Painting (Manet), 1964 (opposite)

Saturday Afternoon, 1995 (above)
Landscape, 1996 (opposite above)
Picasso's Head, 1995 (opposite below)

Saturday Afternoon (1995) was inspired by a photograph of Kiki de Montparnasse by the American artist Man Ray. Kiki, a French artist's model, was Man Ray's companion in Paris from 1922 to 1926. The photograph, *Noire et blanche* (1926), shows Kiki's head lying sideways on a reflective surface. I thought of similar images of women's heads in *The Turkish Bath* (1863) by Ingres and in *The Blue Eyes* (1935) by Matisse. One Saturday afternoon, I made a drawing of the three images, Ingres on the left, Matisse on the right, Man Ray between them. The drawing became the study for the oil painting, completed several weeks later on another Saturday afternoon.

School of Gauguin, 1993 (above)
School of Modigliani 2, 1988 (opposite)

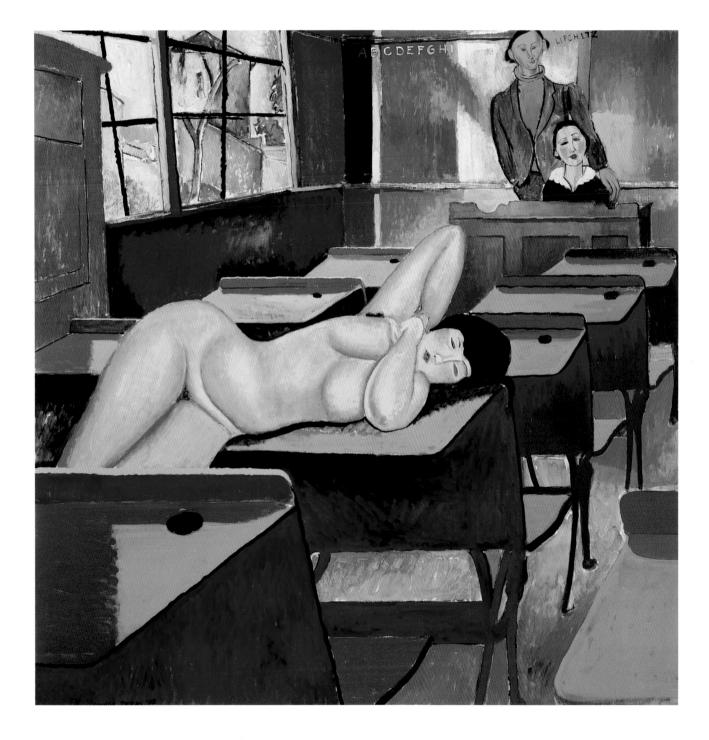

FACULTY OF THE DESSAU BAUHAUS, 1926: LEFT TO RIGHT, HINNERK SCHEPER, GEORG MUCHE, LÁSZLÓ MOHOLY-NAGY, HERBERT BAYER, JOOST SCHMIDT, WALTER GROPIUS, MARCEL BREUER, WASSILY KANDINSKY, PAUL KLEE, LYONEL FEININGER, GUNTA STÖLZL, OSKAR SCHLEMMER.

Art Deco School, 1993 (above)
Bauhaus School, 1986 (opposite)

Mayakovsky in Delft, 1980 (opposite)
The Red Hammer, 1987 (below)

LIST OF PLATES

Measurements are given in inches and centimeters, height x width.

Page 13: *School of Rembrandt*, 1989
Oil on canvas, 30 x 42 (76.2 x 106.7)
Albrecht-Kemper Museum of Art,
    St. Joseph, Missouri, W. Dean Eckert
    Bequest. Photo Edward Peterson Jr.

Page 14: *Vermeer's "Lady Seated at a
    Virginal," the Lady Removed*, 1999
Oil on canvas, 20 x 18 (50.8 x 45.7)
Collection of the artist. Photo Edward
    Peterson Jr.

Page 17: *School of Athens*, 1998
Oil on canvas, 48 x 36 (122 x 91.5)
The Bellagio Gallery of Fine Art, MGM
    Grand/Mirage Resorts, Inc., Las Vegas,
    Nevada. Photo Edward Peterson Jr.

Pages 18–19: *The Triumph of Art*, 1990
Oil on canvas, 54 x 96 (137.2 x 243.9)
Collection Paul, Weiss, Rifkind, Wharton &
    Garrison, LLP, New York. Photo Edward
    Peterson Jr.

Page 20: *L'Ecole des Beaux-Arts*, 1991
Oil on canvas, 58 x 70 (147.3 x 177.8)
Collection George Freedman, Sydney,
    Australia. Photo Edward Peterson Jr.

Page 21: *Le Musée d'Orsay*, 1997
Oil on canvas, 70 x 58 (177.8 x 147.3)
Collection Martin Lindstrom, Sydney,
    Australia. Photo Edward Peterson Jr.

Page 22: *Del Sarto Canaletto Titian*, 1995
Oil on canvas, 40 x 32 (101.6 x 81.3)
Collection of the artist. Photo Edward
    Peterson Jr.

Page 23: *The Studio of Jacques-Louis David*,
    1996
Oil on canvas, 70 x 58 (177.8 x 147.3)
Courtesy Pavel Zoubok Gallery, New York.
    Photo Edward Peterson Jr.

Pages 24–25: *Boston Pastime*, 1988
Oil on canvas, 48 x 120 (122 x 304.8)
Collection Nutter, McClennen & Fish,
    Boston. Photo Edward Peterson Jr.

Page 26: *School of Velázquez*, 1987
Oil on canvas, 70 x 60 (177.8 x 152.4)
Private collection. Photo Edward
    Peterson Jr.

Page 27: *Easel Painting*, 1993
Oil on canvas, 72 x 48 (182.9 x 122)
Collection of the artist. Photo Edward
    Peterson Jr.

Pages 28–29: *The Landscape Painter*, 1993
Oil on canvas, 24 x 32 (61 x 91.5)
Collection of the artist. Photo Edward
    Peterson Jr.

Pages 30–31: *Auction*, 1980
Oil on canvas, 40 x 50 (101.6 x 127)
Collection Mrs. Samuel J. Krasney, Pepper
    Pike, Ohio. Photo Kirk Winslow

Page 33: *Composition with Millet*, 1963
Oil on canvas, 40 x 30 (101.6 x 76.2)
Collection of the artist. Photo Edward
    Peterson Jr.

Page 34: *School of Caravaggio*, 1984
Oil on canvas, 30 x 42 (86.4 x 106.7)
Collection Garland and Suzanne Marshall,
    Clayton, Missouri. Photo Edward
    Peterson Jr.

Page 35: *The Spanish School*, 1993
Oil on canvas, 32 x 34 (81.3 x 86.4)
Hotel Beau Rivage, Biloxi, Mississippi,
    Collection of MGM Grand/Mirage
    Resorts, Inc., Las Vegas, Nevada.
    Photo Edward Peterson Jr.

Page 36: *The Caravaggio Saint
    Matthew*, 1979
Oil on canvas, 90 x 72 (228.6 x 182.9)
Evansville Museum of Arts, History, and
    Science, Evansville, Indiana. Photo Kirk
    Winslow

Page 37: *Terborch Silver Dresses*, 1979
Oil and aluminum silver paint on paper,
    20.5 x 24 (52 x 61)
Collection of the artist. Photo Edward
    Peterson Jr.

Pages 38–39: *Bruegel Tiles*, 2002
Oil on canvas, 15 x 22 (38.1 x 55.9)
Collection of the artist. Photo Edward
Peterson Jr.

Page 40: *Ellen and George*, 1983
Oil on canvas, 16 x 18 (40.7 x 45.7)
Collection Ann Houston, Indianapolis,
Indiana. Photo Hadley W. Fruits

Page 41: *Portrait of Mary Ellen Andrews in
a Renaissance Landscape*, 1972
Oil on canvas, gold leaf, and wood frame,
17 x 13 (43.2 x 33) framed
Collection Mary Ellen Andrews, New York.
Photo Edward Peterson Jr.

Page 42: *An English Quilt*, 1971
Oil on canvas, 31.5 x 27.5 (80 x 70)
Collection of the artist. Photo Edward
Peterson Jr.

Page 43: *An English Painting*, 1965
Oil on canvas, 60 x 50 (152.4 x 127)
Collection Paul, Weiss, Rifkind, Wharton
& Garrison, LLP, New York. Photo
Edward Peterson Jr.

Page 44: *Occidental Rug*, 1970
Oil on canvas, 28 x 23 (71.1 x 58.4)
Collection of the artist. Photo Edward
Peterson Jr.

Page 45: *Composition with Women*, 1966
Oil on canvas, 50 x 40 (127 x 101.6)
Evansville Museum of Arts, History, and
Science, Evansville, Indiana. Photo
courtesy Evansville Museum of Arts,
History, and Science

Pages 46–47: *School of Courbet*, 1988
Oil on canvas, 44 x 60 (111.8 x 152.4)
Private collection. Photo Edward
Peterson Jr.

Page 48: *Multiple Frans Hals*, 1963
Oil on canvas, 40 x 36 (101.6 x 91,5)
Weatherspoon Art Museum, The University
of North Carolina at Greensboro, Gift of
Mr. Robert C. Scull, 1981. Photo Dan
Smith

Page 49: *Composition in Red and
Black*, 1972
Oil on canvas, 19¾ x 15¾ (50 x 40)
Collection of the artist. Photo Edward
Peterson Jr.

Pages 2 (detail), 50–51: *Sebastian in the
Kitchen*, 1977
Oil on canvas, 20 x 24 (50.8 x 61)
Collection George Freedman, Sydney,
Australia. Photo Greg Weight

Pages 52–53: *Vermeer in Florence*, 1976
Oil on paper map, 17 x 25 (43.2 x 63.5)
Private collection. Photo John
Credland

Page 54: *Auto Portrait*, 1971
Oil on canvas, 19⅝ x 23⅝ (50 x 60)
Collection of the artist. Photo Edward
Peterson Jr.

Page 55: *Double Dutch Landscape*, 1963
Oil on canvas, 51 x 45 (129.5 x 114.3)
Miami University Art Museum, Oxford,
Ohio, Gift of Mrs. Robert B. Mayer and
Children. In memory of Robert B. Mayer,
1979.P.8.8. Photo courtesy Miami
University Art Museum

Page 57: *Deem Vermeer*, 1974
Oil on canvas, 16 x 13 (40.7 x 33)
University of Southern Indiana, Evansville,
Kenneth P. McCutchan Bequest

Pages 58–59: *Vermeer Palette*, 1983
Oil on L-shaped canvas, 20 x 26 (50.8 x 66)
Collection Diane Meyer Simon, Montecito,
California. Photo Hadley W. Fruits

Page 60: *A Stool, a Chair, and a Map*, 2003
Oil on canvas, 54 x 42 (137.2 x 106.7)
Courtesy Pavel Zoubok Gallery, New York.
Photo Edward Peterson Jr.

Page 61: *Vermeer Detail*, 2003
Oil on canvas, 18 x 14 (45.7 x 35.6)
Courtesy Pavel Zoubok Gallery, New York.
Photo Edward Peterson Jr.

Pages 62–63: *The Art of Painting*,
2002 (diptych)
Oil on canvas, each canvas 35 x 40
(89 x 101.6)
Courtesy Pavel Zoubok Gallery, New York.
Photo Edward Peterson Jr.

Pages 64–65: *New York Artist in His
Studio/Vermeer's "Artist in His Studio,"*
1979 (diptych)
Oil on canvas, each canvas 53 x 44
(134.6 x 111.8)
Manney Collection, New York. Photo Kirk
Winslow

Pages 66–67: *Seven Vermeer Corners,* 1999
Oil on canvas, 50 x 86 (127 x 218.5)
Collection Wellington Management
Company, Boston. Photo Edward
Peterson Jr.

Pages 68–69: *An American Vermeer,*
1970–71
Oil on canvas, 42 x 93 (106.7 x 236.2)
Indianapolis Museum of Art, Gift of the
Contemporary Art Society. Photo courtesy
Indianapolis Museum of Art

Page 70: *Vermeer's Red Rug,* 1981
Oil on canvas, 44 x 60 (111.8 x 152.4)
Collection David and Lynn Walker,
Louisville, Kentucky. Photo Kirk
Winslow

Page 71: *Study for Vermeer's "Concert"
with Two Figures Removed,* 1997
Oil on paper, 21¼ x 22 (54 x 55.9)
Collection Walter and Nancy Liedtke,
Bedford, New York. Photo Edward
Peterson Jr.

Pages 72–73: *How to Paint a Vermeer,* 1981
Oil on canvas, 44 x 66 (111.8 x 167.7)
Collection Marguerita S. Putnam and
Jedediah Wheeler, New York. Photo
Kirk Winslow

Page 74: *The Red Chair,* 2002
Oil on canvas, 24 x 24 (61 x 61)
Courtesy Pavel Zoubok Gallery, New York.
Photo Edward Peterson Jr.

Page 75: *Painting Perspective,* 2001
Oil on canvas, 40 x 72 (101.6 x 183)
Courtesy Pavel Zoubok Gallery, New York.
Photo Edward Peterson Jr.

Page 76: *Vermeer's "Music Lesson" with the
Figures Removed,* 1998
Oil on canvas, 24 x 24 (61 x 61)
Collection David Littlejohn, Kensington,
California. Photo Edward Peterson Jr.

Page 77: *Vermeer's Easel,* 1999
Oil on canvas, 42 x 36 (106.7 x 91.5)
Private collection. Photo Edward
Peterson Jr.

Page 78: *Extended Vermeer,* 2000
Oil on canvas, 40 x 36 (101.6 x 91.5)
Collection Linda Cheverton Wick and
Walter Wick, Connecticut. Photo Edward
Peterson Jr.

Page 79: *Woman with a Water Pitcher,* 2002
Oil on canvas, 18 x 16 (45.7 x 40.6)
Courtesy Pavel Zoubok Gallery, New York.
Photo Edward Peterson Jr.

Page 80: *Vermeer Interior without
Figure,* 1970
Oil on wood panel in gesso molded frame,
27⅛ x 23⅜ (69 x 59.5) framed
Collection Ann Rubin, Naples, Florida.
Photo Carl J. Thome

Page 81: *Vermeer's Chair,* 1994
Oil on canvas, 28 x 24 (71.1 x 61)
Collection Mr and Mrs. David Glew, New
York. Photo Edward Peterson Jr.

Page 83: *George Washington and His
Portrait,* 1972
Oil on canvas, 23⅝ x 19¾ (60 x 50)
Collection of the artist. Photo Edward
Peterson Jr.

Page 84: *George Washington in White
Face,* 1974
Oil on canvas, 7⅞ x 6⅞ (20 x 15)
JP Morgan Chase Bank Art Collection.
Photo Edward Peterson Jr.

Page 85: *George Washington Shaving,* 1992
Oil on canvas and wood frame, 16¼ x 14
(41.3 x 35.6) framed
Private collection. Photo Edward
Peterson Jr.

Page 86: *Mona Lisa Washington,* 1972
Pencil on paper, 19 x 12 (48.3 x 30.5)
Collection Roberta Rymer Balfe, Santa Fe,
New Mexico

Page 87: *George Washington Vermeer,* 1974
Oil on canvas, 31½ x 27½ (80 x 70)
Collection of the artist. Photo Edward
Peterson Jr.

Page 88: *American Express,* 2000
Oil on canvas, 12 x 11 (30.5 x 28)
Collection of the artist. Photo Edward
Peterson Jr.

Page 89: *Random House,* 1975
Oil on canvas, 7⅞ x 11⅞ (20 x 30)
Collection Nancy Drosd and Charles
    Schwartz, New York. Photo Edward
    Peterson Jr.

Page 90: *Ruscha,* 2001
Oil on canvas, 12 x 11 (30.5 x 28)
Collection of the artist. Photo Edward
    Peterson Jr.

Page 91: *A Letter to Mark Tobey,* 1959
Oil on canvas, 48 x 36 (122 x 91.5)
Whereabouts unknown

Page 92: *An American Rug,* 1970
Oil on canvas, 50½ x 39½
    (128.3 x 100.3)
Evansville Museum of Arts, History, and
    Science, Evansville, Indiana. Photo
    courtesy Evansville Museum of Arts,
    History, and Science

Page 93: *Bingham Ceiling,* 1993
Oil on canvas, 70 x 58 (177.8 x 147.3)
Private collection. Photo Edward
    Peterson Jr.

Page 94: *Hudson River School,* 1995
Oil on canvas, 42 x 54 (106.7 x 137.2)
Courtesy Pavel Zoubok Gallery, New York.
    Photo Edward Peterson Jr.

Page 95: *Eakins and Apples,* 1981
Oil on canvas, 36 x 42 (91.5 x 106.7)
Bank of America Art Collection. Photo Kirk
    Winslow

Page 96: *MacDowell Colony,* 1978
Oil on canvas, 20 x 18 (50.8 x 45.7)
Collection Martin Sinkoff, New York.
    Photo Edward Peterson Jr.

Page 97: *A Painting for Babies,* 1970/1980
Oil on canvas, 22 x 20 (55.9 x 50.8)
Evansville Museum of Arts, History, and
    Science, Evansville, Indiana. Photo
    Edward Peterson Jr.

Page 98: *Portrait on Demand,* 1992
Oil on canvas, 16 x 20 (40.7 x 50.8)
Collection of the artist. Photo Edward
    Peterson Jr.

Page 99: *Edward and Jo Hopper,* 1995
Oil on canvas, 32 x 42 (81.3 x 106.7)
Courtesy Pavel Zoubok Gallery, New York.
    Photo Edward Peterson Jr.

Page 100: *The Presidents of the United
    States,* 1983
Oil on canvas, 70 x 50 (177.8 x 127)
Manney Collection, New York. Photo Kirk
    Winslow

Page 101: *November Calendar,* 1966
Oil on canvas, 50 x 40 (127 x 101.6)
Whereabouts unknown

Page 102: *Ashcan School,* 1987
Oil on canvas, 40 x 48 (101.6 x 122)
Collection of the artist. Photo Edward
    Peterson Jr.

Page 103: *The Fall of Whistler's
    Mother,* 1969
Oil on canvas, 22 x 25 (55.9 x 63.5)
Manney Collection, New York

Pages 104–5: *Schoolroom,* 1979
Oil on canvas, 34 x 42 (86 x 107)
Collection Dr. Meg Blair, Nantucket,
    Massachusetts. Photo Edward
    Peterson Jr.

Page 107: *Hans Hofmann Vermeer,* 1980
Acrylic on paper, 28 x 22 (71.1 x 55.9)
Collection Paul, Weiss, Rifkind, Wharton &
    Garrison, LLP, New York. Photo Edward
    Peterson Jr.

Pages 4–5 (detail), 108–9: *Everybody's
    Schoolroom,* 1994
Oil on canvas, 34 x 36 (86.4 x 91.5)
Collection Cleary, Gottlieb, Steen
    & Hamilton, New York. Photo Edward
    Peterson Jr.

Pages 110–11: *Cubist Cache,* 1995
Oil on canvas, 44 x 56 (111.8 x 142.2)
Private collection. Photo Edward
    Peterson Jr.

Page 112: *Arshile Gorky and His Mother,* 1989
Oil on canvas, 42 x 36 (106.7 x 91.5)
Collection David and Vivian Campbell,
    Toronto, Canada. Photo Edward
    Peterson Jr.

Page 113: *School of Arshile Gorky,* 1995
Oil on canvas, 24 x 36 (61 x 91.5)
Collection of the artist. Photo Edward
    Peterson Jr.

Page 114: *A Working Painting (Manet),*
1964
Oil on canvas, 42¼ x 36 (107.3 x 91.4)
San Francisco Museum of Modern Art, Gift
of Mr. and Mrs. William C. Janss. Photo
courtesy San Francisco Museum of
Modern Art

Page 115: *Manet Palette,* 1994
Oil on wood, 12 x 16 (30.5 x 40.6)
Collection of the artist. Photo Edward
Peterson Jr.

Page 116: *Saturday Afternoon,* 1995
Oil on canvas, 24 x 35 (61 x 88.9)
Courtesy Pavel Zoubok Gallery, New York.
Photo Edward Peterson Jr.

Page 117: *Landscape,* 1996
Oil on aluminum mounted on wood, 18 x 24
(45.7 x 61)
Collection of the artist. Photo Edward
Peterson Jr.

Page 117: *Picasso's Head,* 1995
Oil on cardboard, 18 x 24 (45.7 x 61)
Collection Reagan and Roberta Upshaw,
Brooklyn, New York. Photo Edward
Peterson Jr.

Page 118: *School of Gauguin,* 1993
Oil on burlap, 22 x 30 (55.9 x 76.2)
Collection A. J. Musia, Evansville, Indiana.
Photo Camera Arts

Page 119: *School of Modigliani 2,* 1988
Oil on canvas, 36 x 36 (91.5 x 91.5)
Courtesy Pavel Zoubok Gallery, New York.
Photo Edward Peterson Jr.

Page 120: *Bauhaus School,* 1986
Oil on canvas, 50 x 50 (127 x 127)
Courtesy Nancy Hoffman Gallery, New
York. Photo Edward Peterson Jr.

Page 121: *Art Deco School,* 1993
Oil on canvas, 34 x 36 (86.4 x 91.5)
Collection of the artist. Photo Edward
Peterson Jr.

Page 122: *The Red Hammer,* 1987
Oil on plywood, metal nails, and metal
scissors, 45 x 45 (114.3 x 114.3)
Collection of the artist. Photo Edward
Peterson Jr.

Page 123: *Mayakovsky in Delft,* 1980
Oil on canvas, 50 x 50 (127 x 127)
Collection of the artist. Photo Edward
Peterson Jr.

Manet Box, 1992
Oil on board, 5 wood panels,
12 x 12 x 12 (30.5 x 30.5 x 30.5)
Collection Neale M. Albert, New York.
Photo Edward Peterson Jr.